The SIMONE BILES Story

THE GIRL WHO DEFIED GRAVITY

The
SIMONE
BILES
Story
THE GIRL WHO
DEFIED GRAVITY
KERIANNE JELINEK

Once upon
a time, in a
small town
called
Columbus,
Ohio, there
was a little
girl named
Simone.

She was full of energy,
always bouncing and
jumping.

Her parents called her a little bundle of joy!
Simone loved to play outside, climb trees, and do cartwheels.

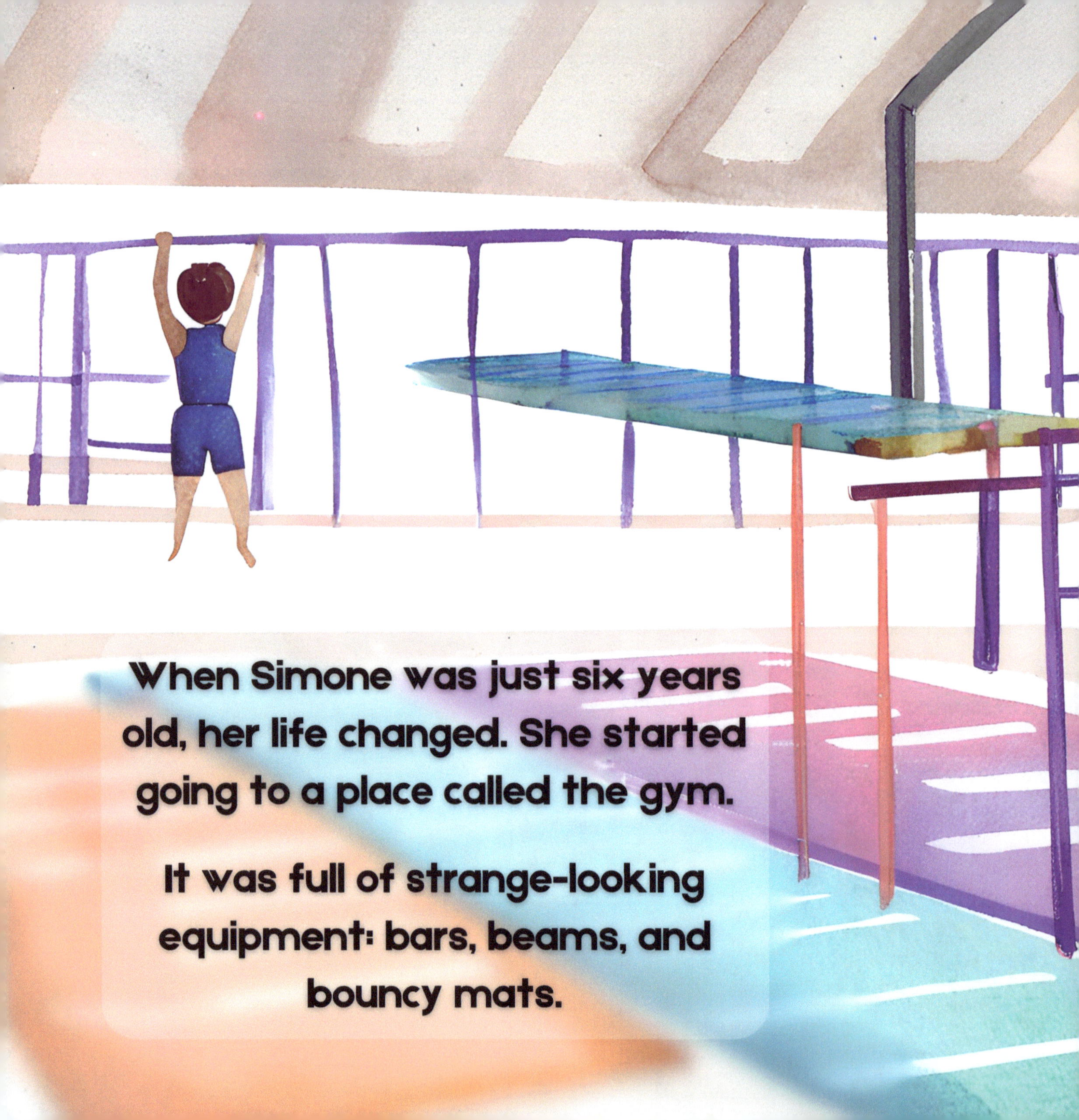

When Simone was just six years old, her life changed. She started going to a place called the gym.

It was full of strange-looking equipment: bars, beams, and bouncy mats.

At first, Simone was scared.

But soon, she realized how much fun it was to flip and fly!

Simone was special.

She could do things that other kids couldn't.
She could twist and turn her body like a
dancer, and she was so strong! Her coaches
were amazed. They said she was a natural.

Training
was hard
work.

Simone had to practice for hours every day.

She missed playing with her friends sometimes, and she got tired.

As Simone grew older, she got better and better.

She won medals at big competitions.

Everyone started calling her a gymnastics superstar!

But Simone never forgot where she came from. She was still the same happy, bouncy girl who loved to play.

One day,
something
very special
happened.

Simone went to a place called Rio de Janeiro, in
a faraway country called Brazil to compete.

There was a big sports competition called the Olympics. People from all over the world came to watch amazing athletes compete.

Simone
was
there
too!

She did flips and twists that made everyone gasp. She won lots of gold medals. She was the best gymnast in the whole world!

But
Simone
didn't
just win
medals.

She showed everyone that
it's okay to be different.

She taught kids that with hard work and a little bit of magic, you can achieve your dreams.

Simone won the most medals out of any other gymnast in history.

She competed in three Olympic Games. Rio de Janiero in 2016, Tokyo in 2020, and at the Paris Olympics in 2024. She holds four gold medals, one silver, and two bronze medals.

Simone Biles is a
real-life superhero.

She can fly through the air, but she's also kind, smart, and funny. And she's proof that anyone can be amazing, if they just believe in themselves.

So, the next time you feel like giving up, remember Simone.

Remember how she practiced hard, never gave up, and became the best.

You can do
AMAZING
THINGS
TOO!

Simone Biles: A Gymnastics Superstar

Simone Biles, born on March 14, 1997 1, is one of the most decorated gymnasts in history. Her journey began at a young age - she was only six years old when she discovered her love for gymnastics during a daycare field trip 3, and from there, her talent shone brightly.

Simone has competed at the highest level, winning numerous medals at the World Championships and Olympics. She is a four-time Olympic gold medalist (2016 Rio Olympics) and a four-time Olympic gold medalist (2020 Tokyo Olympics), and medals in the Paris Olympics 2024. Her impressive medal collection also includes World Championship gold medals on vault, balance beam, floor exercise, and all-around competitions.

Simone's upbringing instilled in her the values of hard work and determination. Raised by her grandparents in Texas, she has always shown a positive attitude and a love for the sport.

Simone Biles is more than just a champion; she is an inspiration to young athletes everywhere.

Naomi Baker/Getty Images

Getty Images

Simone Biles at World Championships

October 5, 2023

https://www.self.com/story/simone-biles-world-championships-gold-medal-2023

Photographer Naomi Baker for Getty Images

Image used under the Creative Common License © 2024
https://creativecommons.org/licenses/by/4.0/